Text and photographs by
Wayne Lynch

Whose Tongue Is This?

WALRUS
B O O K S

To Aubrey, who always makes the sun shine brighter

Edited by Viola Funk
Photography by Wayne Lynch
Interior design by Warren Clark and
    Setareh Ashrafologhalai
Typesetting and illustrations by
    Setareh Ashrafologhalai

Printed in China at 1010 Printing Asia Ltd.

**Library and Archives Canada Cataloguing in
Publication**

Lynch, Wayne
    Whose tongue is this? / text and photographs
by Wayne Lynch.

Includes index.
ISBN 978-1-77050-035-8

    1. Animals--Identification--Juvenile literature.
2. Tongue--Juvenile literature. I. Title.

QL946.L95 2011   j591.4'4   C2010-907276-6

The publisher acknowledges the financial
support of the Canada Council for the Arts,
the British Columbia Arts Council, and the
Government of Canada through the Canada
Book Fund (CBF). Whitecap Books also
acknowledges the financial support of the
Province of British Columbia through the Book
Publishing Tax Credit.

Canada Council   Conseil des Arts
for the Arts   du Canada

BRITISH COLUMBIA
ARTS COUNCIL

11 12 13 14 15   5 4 3 2 1

It's hard to imagine being without a tongue. Humans use their tongues to speak, to whistle, and to play some musical instruments. Best of all, we can use it to lick ice cream off our lips. Some people can even lick the tip of their nose!

If you grab your tongue you will discover that it is slippery and spongy. Most wild animals have a tongue that is very different from ours. Some animals have tongues that are sticky, and some have a tongue as rough as sandpaper. Different animals use their tongues to catch their food or to comb their fur. See if you can figure out who owns the tongues in this book.

I have a very long tongue that I use like a hand to tear off leaves and small branches from trees. The trees try to stop me from eating them by covering their branches with sharp thorns, but my tongue and mouth are as tough as leather. Because I am so tall I can reach branches that are as high as the roof of a house.

Who am I?

3

4

am a giraffe. I live in Africa where there are lions, hyenas, and leopards that would like to eat me. Luckily, I can run faster than any of them, but I can also kick very hard with my feet if they come too close. I am the tallest animal in the world and I can see danger coming from far away.

A mother giraffe gives birth while she is standing, so the first experience that her baby has is dropping to the ground with a thud.

When I am not using my long tongue, I keep it rolled up in a circle so that I don't step on it. My tongue is like a drinking straw that I use to sip the sweet water I find inside flowers. I use my sensitive feet to taste the flower first. When I find some sweet water, I unroll my tongue and suck up the tasty liquid.

Who am I?

I bet you guessed that I am a butterfly. I can't bite or chew because I have no teeth or jaws, and usually my only food is the sweet water inside flowers, called nectar. In some tropical forests, a few butterflies even drink the tears of big animals. My large eyes can see more colors than a human can, and I usually prefer flowers that are orange, red, or yellow.

The wings of a butterfly are covered with colorful scales like the tiles on the roof of a house.

My tongue and the inside of my mouth look scary because they are covered with stiff spines.

My favorite food is fish—I catch them by diving deep into the ocean. Fish are slippery, but the spines on my tongue and on the roof of my mouth point inward and this helps me to hold and swallow my food. On a single dive I sometimes catch 10 fish, which I swallow underwater.

Who am I?

I am a penguin. I can't fly because I don't have wings. Instead, I have stiff flippers that I use like wings to fly underwater. Not all penguins live in places covered with ice and snow. I am a rockhopper penguin, and I live where it rarely snows. I am called a rockhopper because of the funny way I hop with my short legs to climb the cliffs where I nest.

Rockhopper penguins, like most penguins, lay two eggs, and the chicks take two to three months to grow up.

I am a hunter and I usually catch my food by sneaking up close to it and then chasing it. Sometimes when I hunt I get very dirty and covered with mud. My big floppy tongue is rough like sandpaper, and I use my tongue to comb my fur and clean off the dirt. My scratchy tongue also helps me scrape small bits of meat off of bones when I am eating.

Who am I?

14

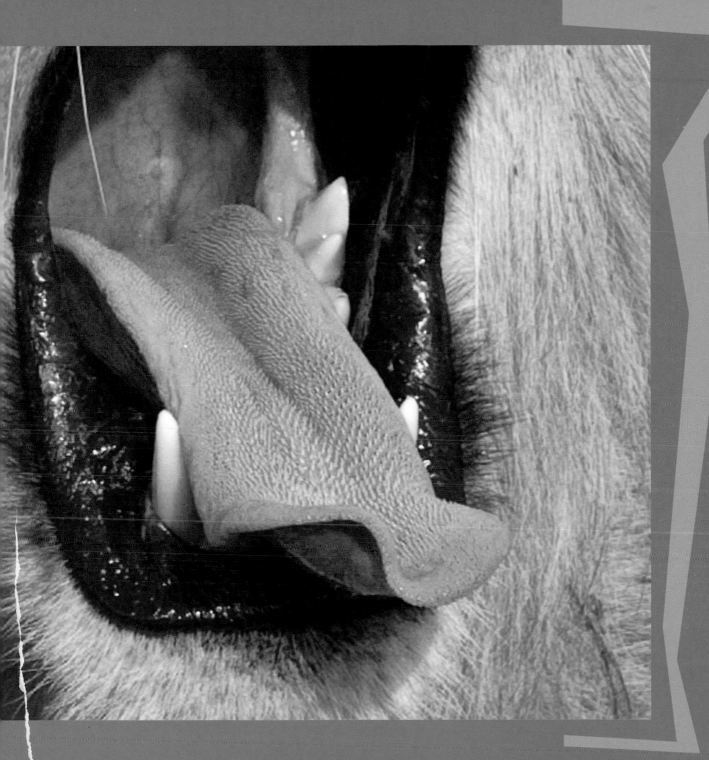

I am a mother lion. I live in Africa, where I hunt zebras, gazelles, and wildebeest to eat. I live in a group, sometimes with 10 other mother lions and their cubs. When my cubs are very small I keep them hidden from other lions, but by the time they are two months old we travel around together as one big family.

A mother lion usually raises one to four cubs at a time. Hyenas are the biggest danger to small cubs.

I bet you think my tongue looks like a juicy pink worm. That is exactly what I hope a fish will think when I wiggle my tongue underwater. When the fish comes over to get a closer look I snap my mouth shut like a trap. I can stay underwater for almost an hour without needing to come up for a breath of air.

Who am I?

I am an alligator snapping turtle and I am the largest freshwater turtle in North America. I can weigh more than an adult human. When I am lying in the mud on the bottom of a lake I am very hard to see, so it's easy to understand how I can fool a fish with my wiggly tongue. Besides fish, I also eat waterbirds, crayfish, snakes, and baby alligators.

Alligator snapping turtles are often caught to be sold as pets, and this has caused them to disappear from many areas.

I live in South America and I have a very funny-looking face. My head is shaped like a narrow tube with ears on it, and my tongue is longer than your arm. I have no teeth, and I use my sticky tongue to lick up ants and termites. When I am eating, I flick my tongue in and out, and in and out, faster than you can count.

Who am I?

I am a giant anteater. I use my strong front legs and large claws to tear apart termite mounds and ant nests, which can sometimes be as hard as cement. My eyes are small and I can't see very well so I use my sensitive nose to find food. My thick fur coat is stiff like straw but it keeps me warm at night. Even in the tropics the nights can be cool.

A mother giant anteater has only one baby at a time, and it rides on her back like a cowboy riding a horse.

25

Even though I have two holes in my nose, I use them only to breathe. I use my tongue to smell. When I want to smell the air I flick my tongue in and out. Odors floating in the air stick to the wet surfaces of my tongue. Then when I suck my tongue back inside my mouth I can decide if the odors come from food or danger, friend or enemy.

Who am I?

I am a type of snake called a garter snake that lives in Canada and the United States. Winter is a dangerous time for me because I can easily freeze to death. So every year before it starts snowing, I search for deep cracks in the ground where I can hide away from the cold. Sometimes many snakes hide in the same big crack, and in spring we all come out together.

Garter snakes eat worms, slugs, insects, salamanders, frogs, toads, and mice.

Index